How to Tell a Woman by Her Handbag

How to Tell a Woman by Her Handbag

Written and Illustrated by

Kathryn Eisman

Andrews McMeel
Publishing, LLC

Kansas City • Sydney • London

 For information, write Andrews McMeel Publishing, LLC, an Andrews McMeel Universal company, 1130 Walnut Street, Kansas City, Missouri 64106.

ISBN-13: 978-0-7407-9133-8
ISBN-10: 0-7407-9133-8

Library of Congress Control Number: 2009936607

10 11 12 13 14 TWP 10 9 8 7 6 5 4 3 2 1

www.andrewsmcmeel.com

Previously published in Australia in 2008 by the Penguin Group
Design by Evi O. © Penguin Group (Australia)
Author photograph © Kathryn Eisman

To Nana Anna Reich,
for showing me what it is to be a lady

MENU
Dirty Secrets
To Do

CONTENTS

INTRODUCTION

Women are divine and mysterious creatures, gracefully dancing their way through life, all the while carrying the weight of the world on their shoulders. To fully understand a woman, don't be distracted by the light-footed skip in her step; look at the actual weight on her shoulder—her handbag.

While a woman's clothing and shoes might change with different moods and seasons, it's her handbag that remains loyal; after all, it is the item literally closest to her heart.

Fashion comes and goes, but a handbag is forever, be it a design classic that will someday become a family heirloom, or an embarrassing reminder of that punk-rock phase you went through. From tiny sequined clutches to enormous diaper bags, and from chrome beauty cases to shabby leather briefcases, they are a record of a woman's journey from childhood to womanhood, all the while remaining true to her girlhood.

From the time your grandmother magically extracted a white hanky from her purse when your nose ran to the day you lovingly pull out photos of grandchildren from a pouch of your own, the handbag is your constant companion and most trusted friend. Only a fool would dare peek inside a woman's bag; it's a place of mystery, the final frontier of female privacy—a place where cherry lip balms are stored and cute bartenders' numbers are secretly deposited.

A peek inside a woman's bag is a peek inside her soul. There's the woman with the bottomless pit of ideas and half-eaten sandwiches who believes chaos is a small price to pay for creativity; she's the free-spirited genius who has a million important calls to make—once she finds her mobile phone, that is.

Then there's the organized femme in whose bag sits a spare toothbrush, mini-deodorant, phone charger, pair of stockings, and everything else she may need to see her through the day (or year). She's the type who is always prepared for any crisis, the type of woman you'd like to be stuck in a bunker with, since she prepares for life like she's going into battle.

Then there is the bag of the sentimental dreamer who's planning her next adventure as she misses her bus stop. She's content to carry a bag filled with knickknacks from holidays gone by, and perfume and photos and trinkets to remind her of her loved ones, rather than prosaic things like her purse and phone. She's a romantic soul with a wildly passionate side and an even wilder temper.

Or there is the "less is more" type; lip gloss, phone, wallet, and keys are all she needs. She's likely to be overly logical and is often accused of having thrown out her heart along with her taxi receipts.

But you needn't go as far as looking at the contents; just one glance at the bag itself will

tell you everything you need to know. Since ancient Egyptian times, when women elaborately embroidered and encrusted their bags with jewels to denote wealth and class, the handbag has been the ultimate status symbol. Look at the revered handmade gold-mesh bags of the nineteenth century and the three-month-long waiting list for the latest Hermès Birkin bag of today. One needn't have asked Jane Birkin, Grace Kelly, or Jackie Kennedy Onassis which bags they carried; their iconic "it girl" status rested on the very handbags that bear their names.

While every woman is unique, this book will reveal the link between a woman's favorite bag and the woman herself. And, with a little practice, you will be able to identify a woman's real purse-onality. Be it your mother, sister, best friend, foe, colleague, or boss, without her having to utter a word, you will understand her aspirations, sensibility, sensuality, style, and sense of humor, not to mention how many dollars and cents she has in the bank.

From the beggar on the street to the Madison Avenue heiress, we are all bag ladies—now it's time to discover exactly which one.

♥

MENU
MENU
MENU

The Handbags

FLORAL STRAW BAG LADY

She's the perfect, perky princess, the optimist, the jolly Pollyanna, the girl who knows things are just as simple as they appear. Since her life is photographed in pink and white, she has no need for those ugly shades of gray.

She makes homemade cards for birthdays and wears a locket around her neck. She collects and dries flowers and writes thank-you notes to her friends.

She possesses a giddy, giggly girlishness men find intoxicating, a perceived innocence that men will fight over to corrupt. Her fresh-faced optimism makes her irresistible to those men, who wish to devour her like an after-dinner mint. Having endured endless dates with women who they've made bitter, they're thrilled to find something so sweet.

She's the homecoming queen who didn't come home on prom night, the girl with squeaky-clean hair and a diary full of dirty secrets.

Her enthusiasm for life makes her a natural flirt, yet she's unaware of just how often she flirts with danger—unwittingly luring the bad-boy types who can't wait to show this prom queen just how much fun she can have slipping off her throne.

PROS

Nothing is as sexy as innocence.

CONS

Even the sweetest fruits can turn bitter. Be careful who takes a bite.

HOLLYWOOD Bag Lady

Jessica Simpson

SUEDE FRINGED BAG LADY

PROS

She's taken the winding road when it would have been so easy to take the straight and narrow.

CONS

She's the mistress of a carefully constructed carelessness.

HOLLYWOOD Bag Lady

Kate Hudson

More boho than hobo, this alternative lass has adopted the hippie lifestyle without sacrificing the "lifestyle" part. She loves to hang around markets with friends, scouting for up-and-coming designers so she can stay ahead of the trends. She's the girl who buys "vintage," not "second hand." She is the girl who spends forty-five minutes getting ready so she can appear not to care what she looks like.

Fringe Femme will date only the brooding bad-boy type: the man who wears faded ripped jeans and fitted vintage rock 'n' roll T-shirts and carries a guitar. He'll have to be a musician, actor, or artist. He'll be her obsession as well as her plaything, a man "chilled" enough to make Fringy feel cool, perhaps overcompensating for her straight-laced days at school.

Fringy wishes she were a love child of famous bohemians, when in reality she's white bread aspiring to be herb focaccia. A dreamer with her head tightly screwed on, she's the hippie with a business degree ready for when her "artistic" phase passes.

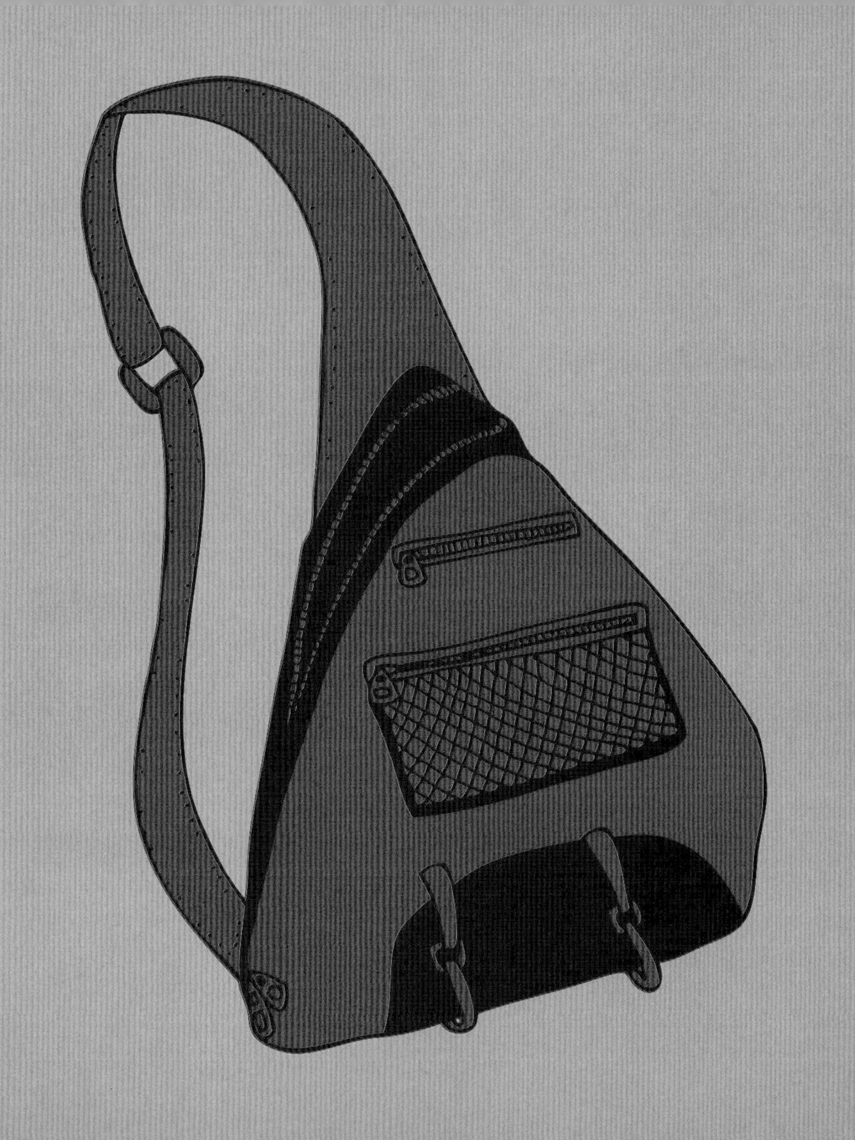

ONE-STRAP MESSENGER BAG LADY

One-Strap Backpack Girl may be strapped for cash, but she's never strapped for ideas. She's the illustrator, the musician, the artist—the type who closes her eyes when listening to music on subways, the type who opens all the windows when driving along highways.

She's the rebel whose mutiny manifests in creation not destruction. She's a hardworking idealist who doodles on the backseats of buses, the girl who goes to concerts alone to inhale the music she craves. She is the girl who wears sneakers to dance parties so she can not only dance but rave.

A subtle femininity lurks beneath that androgynous veneer. She'll never use flirtation to achieve her aims, shunning woman's age-old weapon—lust.

Messenger Bag Girl holds her cards close to her T-shirt-clad chest, preferring to bear the brunt of failure—as well as to savor the taste of victory—all on her own. She would benefit from letting down her guard more often.

Her partner will be her equal, but he needn't be her clone. He'll likely be a coconspirator, an ally, a dreamer unafraid of making this fiercely independent gal a "woman" to his "man."

PROS

She's the quiet rebel who will change the world.

CONS

She's at risk of exhausting herself by lugging around unnecessary angst in that bag of hers. If you share your dreams with the world, the world will share its bounties with the dreamer.

FANNY PACK LADY

PROS

Her wallet is safe and her hands unencumbered; security and freedom are hers.

CONS

She may as well be wearing a chastity belt. We all carry baggage, but who wants it so close to the groin?

HOLLYWOOD Bag Lady

Roseanne Barr

There are only two types of women who would be caught dead wearing a fanny pack. The first is the tourist, the kind who wears white socks with sandals, the type who catches group tour buses with windows so tinted, air-conditioning so strong, and people so familiar that they may as well be watching a DVD at home.

The second sort of woman still turns to 1980s music videos for fashion inspiration and thinks *Vogue* is just the name of a Madonna song. Both kinds of women are living in the past; both need to pass on the fanny pack.

Saddled up with essentials like credit cards, IDs, and cash (clearly no mirror), Fanny Pack Lady is not a huge fan of change—be it in coin form or otherwise. She takes comfort in the familiar and the safe, unaware that this puts her in the high-risk fashion category. While she can appreciate style, she just can't seem to successfully re-create it. Yes, her hands are free to do whatever she pleases, but at what price?

Unless you work in a market and aspire to do so for the rest of your days, you need to ask yourself: Do I really need something accentuating my backside? If the answer is "No," get off the tour bus and walk to your closest handbag store.

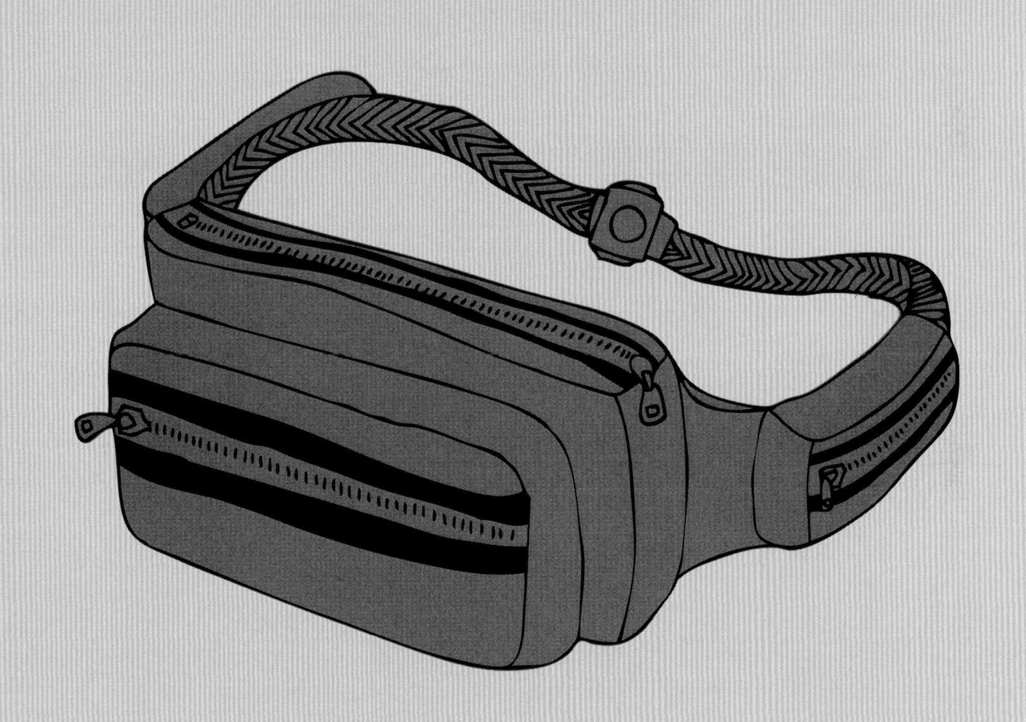

NYLON PRADA BAG LADY

For the woman who surrounds herself with luxury, the nylon Prada bag is a basic necessity that will sit neatly alongside the latest-model BlackBerry, the airiest Italian bed linen, a classic Armani skirt suit, and an imported man with whom she can share a bottle of New Zealand sauvignon blanc.

This dame is so used to the good life she's unaware of how *dolce* her *vita* truly is. So while it's nigh on impossible to get her to 'fess up to being pampered, she does carry herself with the pleasant smile of a satisfied woman.

Perhaps Prada Girl rarely acts like a princess because she believes privilege should serve a purpose. To this end, you're likely to see her sitting on a charitable board or at the head of a boardroom table.

Nylon Prada Lady seeks the same qualities in her man as she does in her handbag: pared-back sturdiness lined with world-class cachet. She expects the best but in return will give the best of herself. She's the kind of woman who'll drink champagne and wash up the glass afterward. While she pretends to be carefree and airy-fairy, in reality she's logical, strategic, and meticulous of mind. If her laugh is light and her walk wistful, make no mistake: She's just playing the ditz. Nylon Prada Lady takes life very seriously indeed, though you'd never know it. She's the sweet, smiling assassin in the softly swinging skirt.

PROS

Just like the bag, she's designer, yet machine-washable.

CONS

She shouldn't forget about the thrills of frivolity.

"IN THE KNOW" BOUTIQUE BAG LADY

PROS

Creativity meets capitalism in an original little package—her.

CONS

When did being unpretentious become so pretentious? There is a profound difference between discovery and possession; just because you found something doesn't mean you own it.

The "In the Know" Bag Lady prides herself on having the latest quirky companion snugly nestled under her arm. Unwilling to reveal her source and relinquish her originality, she'll instead insist that it came from a "quaint little store" somewhere in Europe she knows you'll never visit.

She likes quality and attention to detail and can be even more high-maintenance than her mass-produced designer pals. Her need to have her uniqueness recognized and admired often means Boutique Babe will avoid big-name bags. She won't want to be overshadowed by a brand more powerful than her own.

She's so "in the know" that she can be hard to get to know. As competitive as Boutique Babe can be, when it comes to men she has a soft spot for the humble artisan—the inspired, creative talent whom she discovered and can have all to herself. She needs a man who doesn't threaten her, but, rather, is complementary—just like the turquoise handbag that matches her coral shoes.

Perfumes

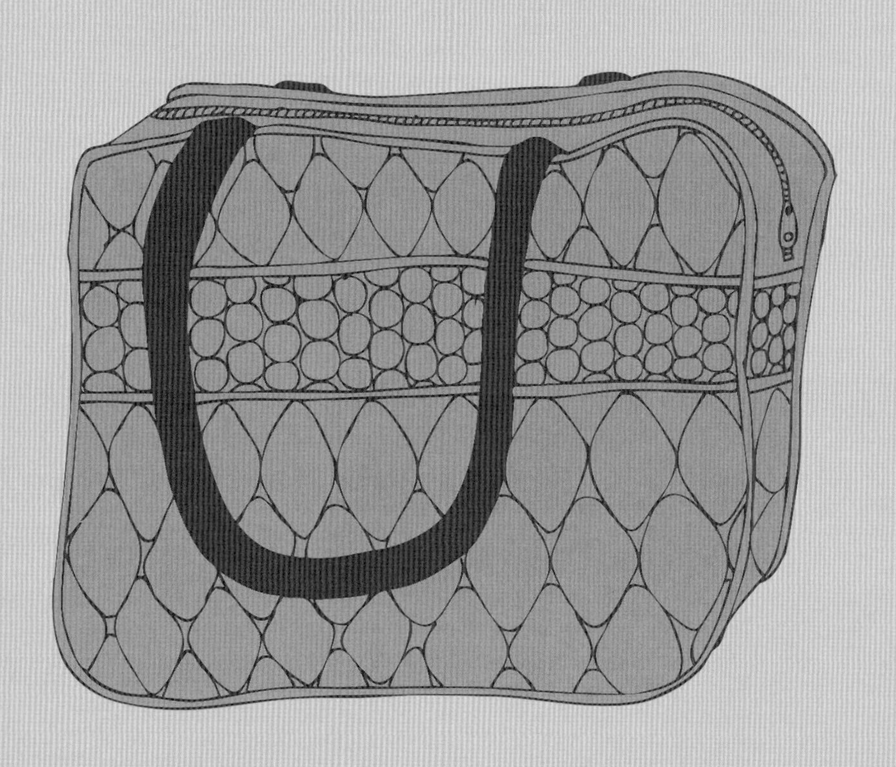

DIAPER BAG LADY

One day she was carrying documents, the next she was accessorizing with her baby's regurgitated dinner. If she had a moment between changing diapers and sterilizing bottles, she might ponder this odd transition . . . it's probably for the best that she doesn't. Forget Madonna, today Diaper Bag Lady knows every word to every song on *Yo Gabba Gabba!*, and considers the Wiggles a musical force to be reckoned with.

Diaper Bag Lady has found an inner strength she never knew existed—and it's even stronger than her beloved bottle of bleach. Once the taker, now the caretaker, she is the student who went on to teach.

Her days of obsessing over minutiae have finally been put to sleep even if she hasn't for the past twelve months. While others may crumble under the pressure, she's discovered the benefits of not having a moment to think about herself. Forced to give up vanity, she is free of the self-interest that causes so much unhappiness. She has discovered the deepest love of all.

Diaper Bag Lady has discovered what really matters underneath all the external fluff. Though she may have cut her long Venus de Milo–esque hair short, she is more feminine than Mother Earth. But she should remember that knowing when to ask for help is a crucial part of being self-sufficient.

PROS

She has discovered that even at its most ugly, reality is more beautiful than artifice.

CONS

She shouldn't forget how she got pregnant in the first place—breasts have a role beyond lactating.

HOLLYWOOD Bag Lady

Kate Winslet

STUDDED BAG LADY

PROS

She's unafraid of staring the ugly truth in the eye, knowing and loving it for what it is.

CONS

She's so prepared for the "worst-case scenario" she wills it upon herself. Lighten up, missy: Optimism is the new black.

HOLLYWOOD Bag Lady

Angelina Jolie

This is a girl who thinks a guy with a stud in his nose will most likely be a stud in the bedroom. Since she's a rebel to the core, she will find an eyebrow ring more romantic than a wedding ring. One represents freedom, the other being trapped, and if there is anything this wild woman fears, it's being tamed. Instead, she's drawn to that which pierces the facade of normality to reveal the flesh of truth.

She gets her sustenance from the hidden recesses of humanity: a weeping guitar or the famished rumbling of a motorbike engine outside her bedroom window.

When Studded Siren says she wants to be put in her place, she isn't talking about picket-fenced suburbia. She doesn't seek a man who'll protect her, rather one with whom she can explore her darker side. Emotionally, she can be satisfied only with an all-encompassing, hungry love that leaves her starved and begging for more.

Studded Siren has enough passion to conquer the world, even if she chooses to use it in the "underworld." Too much time listening to that negative voice in her head, however, and she'll bury her desire so deep it'll buckle under the pressure and mutate into anger and frustration.

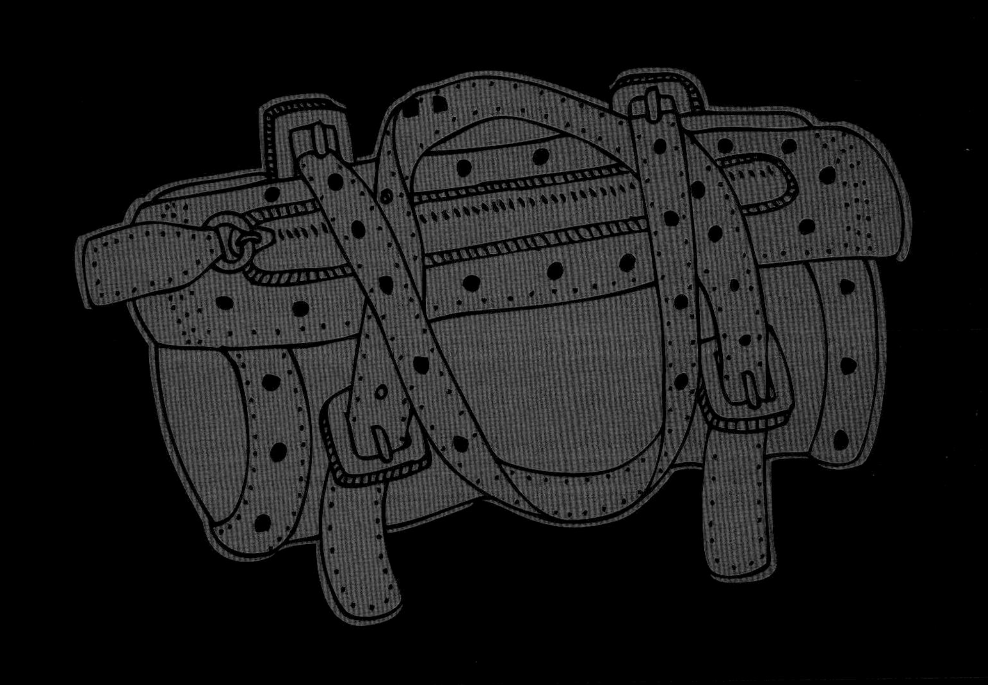

CANVAS TOTE LADY

The girl is carefree; the bag looks like a freebie—they're a perfect match in an imperfect world. At school she was the girl you invited over to play when your best friend was on vacation. Much like the bag itself, she's never been a "must-have" item, nor will she be thrown away next season; she's far too middle-of-the-road to ignite so passionate a response—a point that both comforts and frustrates her. She is at peace with the knowledge that while she'll never hear men gasp as she walks into a room, she'll never hear them gag either.

Though her life may be as mild and muted as a watercolor painting, when it comes to matters of the heart she's part of the "realist school." Canvas Kid is often too practical to ever consider pursuing her elusive masterpiece. As a result, unlike other women, she won't be left hanging on the wall at age forty.

She's an every-woman in search of a man with a good heart, paternal warmth, and just enough character to color her life without saturating it. She'll want someone sturdy whom she can throw in the washing machine, along with the bag, and be safe in the knowledge that they'll both come out just fine.

PROS

Her ideal of love is purely based on loyalty, and she is loyal to the purity of love.

CONS

No matter how sturdy a "bag" is, put it through the wringer too often and the wear and tear will show. She needs to take some time out to indulge in fantasy . . . it is a necessary part of reality.

HOLLYWOOD Bag Ladies

Reese Witherspoon
Jennifer Garner

LOUIS VUITTON GRAFFITI BAG LADY

PROS

She has a healthy sense of adventure and a willingness to look at both sides of the coin.

CONS

She carries only $50 bills. Rebellion is just another form of conformity.

HOLLYWOOD Bag Lady

Kelly Osbourne

This was so "of the moment" that its chicness lasted only that long. The women who invested in the Graffiti Bag should get someone else to manage their finances. Graffiti Gal is a rebellious trend follower, if such a contradiction exists. Sure, she looks punk, but she has the heart of a Rodeo Drive shopper. This girl can afford limos but drives an old Merc; she can afford prêt-à-porter but wears vintage. Drawn to an upscale-downtown style of dressing, she spends a fortune so she can look dirt cheap. Between her Ksubi jeans, her Sass and Bide top, and her Marc Jacobs heels, this little rocker is set to roll.

Graffiti Gal carries around a lot of angst in her expensive scribbled bag. Her sheltered background has made the underground world seem intoxicatingly alluring. But although she may visit dark places, she will never live there. She longs for stimulation and has the shortest of attention spans. Gritty Graffiti Gal finds peace in the absence of quiet.

Her boy must ooze cool to the point of arrogance and be wealthy enough to afford designer distressed jeans. He'll be a spontaneous guy who'll scribble his black magic all over her white life.

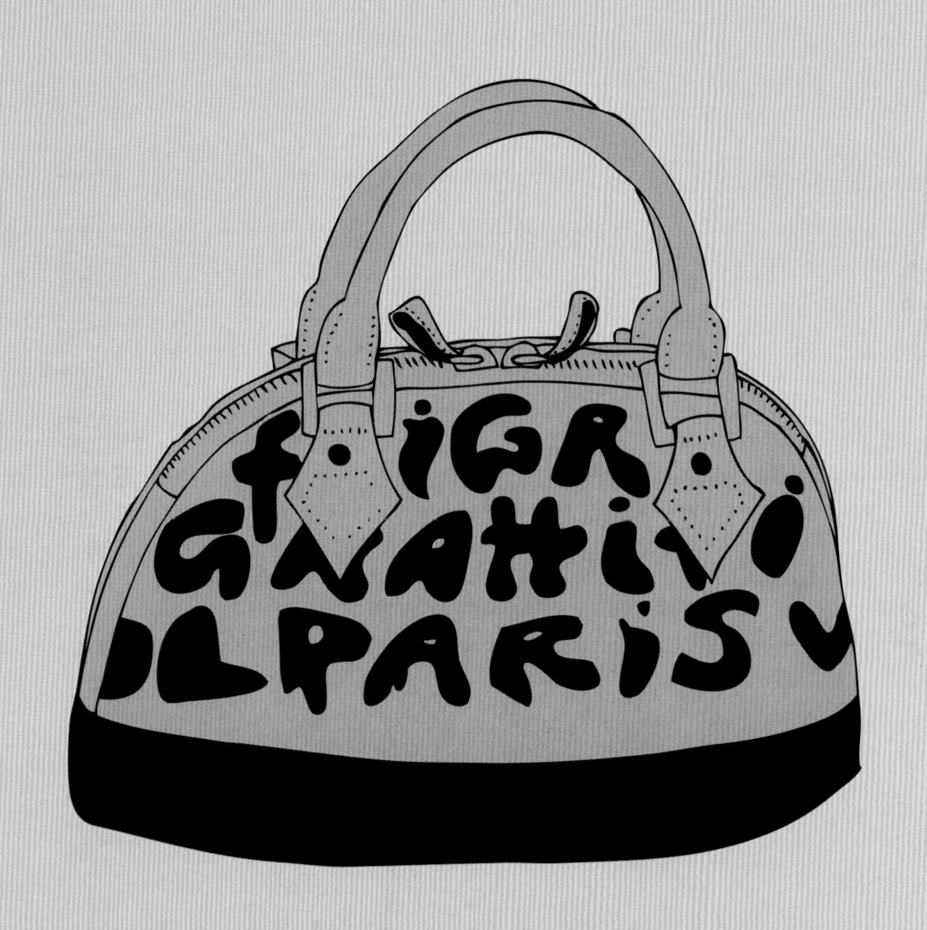
PARIS

HIKING BACKPACK LADY

She goes where the wind and her discount round-the-world ticket take her. Energized by the unexpected, she's on a quest to get lost in order to find herself. In this way, she's running toward her true self by running away from it. Backpack Girl has an insatiable appetite for adventure and a desire to experience anything and everything that is on offer, if only to tick it off her long list. She is open to the world and, as such, the world has opened itself to her.

Though she may be lost on this planet, she is no lost soul. Instead, she connects to each moment, each differing landscape, smiling face, culture, and creature she encounters. It's as if her heart were beating in unison with the planet.

She's often mistaken for a loner, though this is rarely the case. While she reads *Lonely Planet*, she doesn't see the world that way. In truth, she seeks intimacy more fiercely than most; it's just that her love is not the "forever" kind. With each crimson sunset she watches dissolve into a new horizon, with each silent stroll through a frenetic market, she is having a fling with the universe.

Though her backpack may weigh down her golden, muscular shoulders, she travels light—greedy only for adventure.

PROS

She experiences many lives while most people barely live one.

CONS

Without strings attached, people fall down.

DESIGNER FAKE LADY

PROS

While she's faking who she is, at least she's got good taste when it comes to choosing whom to imitate.

CONS

The only person she's kidding is herself.

Designer Fake Girl is all about getting more bang for fewer bucks. She's a true egalitarian who believes everyone should be able to carry a thousand-dollar bag but shouldn't have to pay more than fifty bucks for the privilege.

She's part scavenger, part style queen. The girl will feverishly hunt through sale racks for the "bargain find" that she'll wear to an event where she'll insist on drinking only French champagne.

While it'd be easy to write her off as having little style and no substance, that wouldn't be fair. Designer Fake Girl thinks she doesn't need a "special" price tag in order to make her feel that way. Or, rather, her bank manager thinks that. The sheer chutzpah necessary to pull off pretending to be something she's not shows strength of character.

Her bag may be a fake, but her disloyalty is genuine. Sure, she could invest in a first-class romance or friendship, but why settle for one high-quality item when you can have fifteen cheap imitations for the same price?

She may be fickle when it comes to matters of the heart, but her eternal quest to be *tout le* rage makes her a lively dinner date and a fascinating creature in her own right. She will make you laugh, the bag's blatantly substandard craftsmanship will make you cry, and the whole evening won't cost a pretty penny. Now, isn't that what they call real fun?

JUICY COUTURE
JUICY COUTURE

JUICY COUTURE LADY

She's the trendster in the hipster jeans, showing her "adoring public" a little more butt than they bargained for. Her personality is as colorful as her lemon-yellow skin-tight singlet and as subtle as her pink Swarovski crystal covered mobile phone.

She loves looking girly, yet despite the many hours spent grooming herself, she always manages to look slightly un-kempt. She'll be the one randomly interjecting the word "like" into her sentences. "Like, I just want to, like, get back to, like, my roots." And that's just her talking to her colorist at the hair salon.

She's opinionated and will make a point of making a point, if only to exercise her right to have it. From which bars rock to which brands of jeans flop, she knows all the important stuff. The deepest thing about this girl is her neckline, and her attention span is shorter than her dress.

She loves to get down on the dance floor "like" she's in a gangsta-rap video clip. With moves so smooth, she can't quite work out why the cameras aren't rolling. While Juicy Couture Girl is often accused of being superficial, she's actually more spiritual than she appears. Just ask her Kabbalah and Scientology teachers.

PROS

She lives out loud and in full color.

CONS

Being cool is about not needing to be.

HOLLYWOOD Bag Lady

Paris Hilton

MAGAZINE FREEBIE LADY

PROS

A genuine gal in
a pool of poseurs.

CONS

She's too consumed with trying to be something to actually be something.

While she may look in *Vogue*, she never quite looks "in vogue." Yes, it came free with the magazine, but at a high price to taste. Charmingly clasping her freebie as she skips down the street, she never stops to question why magazines don't feature their own giveaway bags in their fashion spreads.

She has champagne taste on a club-soda budget. She's the budding socialite who catches a yellow cab to red-carpet events. Public transport is her only financially viable means of arriving, so it's little wonder she'll go along to the opening of a car door. Her evenings are spent snacking on complimentary hors d'oeuvres at events while the sole item in her fridge is a carton of spoiled eggs.

Freebie Bag Babe is an aspiring actress/dancer/journalist/whatever. *Aspiring* is the defining word here. Her other aspirations may include snagging the heartthrob she'd love to date or dropping those stubborn ten pounds of extra weight. In spite of her starry-eyed gaze, she is a good-hearted girl and a loyal friend.

COSMO

DECREPIT BRIEFCASE LADY

Rushing through life in a panic, she often forgets why she is in such a hurry. She'll burst into a room only to wonder aloud what she was looking for.

In the office she's all work and no play. At the office Christmas party she's a no-show, believing that one's work should stand for itself. Little does she know that networking would increase her net worth.

At school her projects were never the neatest but always the most original. In college she didn't get asked out on many dates and instead discovered love by reading the poetry of Rumi blissfully alone. She's not the sexiest of women, but while all the other girls were spending their time grooming themselves in the mirror, she was grooming her mind.

Now, her wit is her weapon, and her quirky outlook is more refreshing than iced tea. This woman is a surprise only the worthy will discover. Her perfect partner will be the sort who picks up a book with a worn dust jacket, seeing it not as lackluster but as a classic.

Decrepit Briefcase Girl has made a small and wonderful world for herself, with a quiet corner to call her own and a broken desk chair as her throne. Her man will love her for her spirit rather than her shape, but she'll never feel the burn or the rush of a man loving her only for what he sees.

PROS

A deck of cards with hearts all the way through.

CONS

She's starved for attention while she eats humble pie.

HOLLYWOOD Bag Lady

Ugly Betty

GOLD MESH PURSE LADY

PROS

Her beauty is her vigor.

CONS

Sometimes she's too busy glowing to notice she hasn't paid the electricity bill. Remember, you can dance all night, but don't let your dreams twirl past you.

HOLLYWOOD Bag Lady

Kate Moss

Gold dripping from one finger and sweat dripping from her brow—that's the Gold Mesh Gal. She may not have been alive during the roaring 1920s when the bag first appeared, but her youthful exuberance will keep her in her twenties forever.

The purse of choice in the days of society soirees had its comeback when the world was struck by disco fever, and, like the purse itself, this gal is a melting pot of old-world glamour and retro glitz. She's a party girl who likes getting down and dirty in the most genteel of places. Lively and enthusiastic, she will greet you with a smile, seduce you with a wink, steal your heart with her broken laughter, and forget you with a careless flick of her wrist.

From the vintage purses she found in tiny flea markets to the muso boyfriend she found in a drunken state, Gold Mesh Gal has discovered her greatest treasures in the most unlikely places. She's reluctant to turn down any party invitation; consequently, the only thing she's missing out on is a good night's sleep.

In her apartment is an eclectic mix of secondhand furniture that she's painted cobalt blue, a rusty birdcage she found in her landlord's basement, and an unreal record collection. She picks up these secret splendors with a heart of gold, not a platinum Amex, and that just adds to their value.

FENDI BAGUETTE LADY

This is the perfect accessory for the woman who'd prefer to wear a breadstick than eat one, someone for whom the only acceptable topping for a baguette setting would be a three-carat diamond. Sure, her carbohydrate-free diet is restricted, but Baguette Lady's shopping appetite is insatiable. Her personal trainer may have warned her off rich Italian dishes, but he didn't say anything about not dishing out for Italian designers.

The Fendi Baguette was once the ultimate in glamour, and though Baguette Lady may have put away her prima purse for the present, she's just waiting until it's her time to shine again.

Her taste is impeccable, yet whimsical. She pines for pastel-pink silk curtains and whitewashed wooden floors. Her home is characterized by the sort of girly glamour that requires a couple of full-time housekeepers to maintain. By her bed she'll have a copy of *The Bombshell Manual*, vanilla-scented hand cream, and a hot-pink leather Smythson diary in which she can jot down her dreams.

While she has a sweet nature, she carries herself with such self-satisfaction that one might believe she has a baguette stuck somewhere else other than under her arm. But for all the self-importance, the vanity, and the nail varnish, she does make life seem a little prettier, a little lighter, and a little brighter.

PROS

For all the little girls out there, it's nice to know that Barbie is alive and well.

CONS

The baguette's long thin shape doesn't leave much room for depth.

HOLLYWOOD Bag Lady

Catherine Zeta-Jones

CORPORATE BRIEFCASE LADY

PROS

She's become the man
she wanted to marry.

CONS

No man wants
to marry himself.

HOLLYWOOD Bag Lady

Jodie Foster

She speaks in succinct sentences and will adorn neither her vocabulary nor her office with flowery decorations. She's the "let's get the job done before we have fun" type, although invariably the jobs are never ending and the fun never beginning. She works harder, smarter, and faster than her male peers and always insists that she's ready to do more. Not one to take no for an answer, her way of dealing with obstacles is to enlist a bulldozer. Since she's had to fight her way to the top, she has little sympathy for pretty young things or handsome charmers who come and go with the office mail.

She hides her femininity beneath a minimalist Calvin Klein suit, rarely flaunting it, not even when it would help her in her pursuit of power. Instead, she remains guarded, knowing that in the corporate world one stiletto step out of line could result in her getting the boot.

She's so used to fighting for what she wants that she's forgotten how to just ask for it nicely. She's too busy moving forward to deal with the present or the past. Instead, she works till dark, comes home, pours herself an amber-colored drink, and then closes her heavy lids. She knew that on her way up the corporate ladder there'd be many rungs to climb and people to step over, but she was unprepared for how lonely it would be at the top.

BAMBOO CANE HANDLE LADY

This bag suggests a controlled strain of sophistication and represents the woman who is short of nothing (except perhaps time). Cane Handle Lady is no stranger to being disciplined by the cane. She probably went to a strict all-girls boarding school or now lives as if she were in one. She's meticulous, exacting, and can cut through flesh with a glance.

From her crisp white-walled apartment to her favorite Sergio Rossi black pumps, Madame Cane is at once luxurious and pared back. She expects her shirts to be starched, her floors to be polished, her staff to be nervous, and the bill to be expensive. Who knew that keeping things simple cost so much money?

If you have her as a boss (a role you'll often find her in), don't bother opening your mouth to speak unless you have something important to say and fewer than five words to say it in. As a friend, she's loyal and honest but can sometimes be harsher than the scotch she drinks on the rocks at the end of a long day. If she thinks your party is a failure, she won't be making small talk; she'll be in a cab on her way home.

Madame Cane's man will need to be as polished and punctual as her stainless-steel Cartier Tank Francaise watch in order for her to slip hers off and waste some delicious time with him.

PROS

She's more organized than her beloved Palm Pilot—and a lot less flighty.

CONS

When does self-control become self-confinement? Love breathes in confusion; don't suffocate it with order.

QUILTED CHANEL LADY

PROS

She's always perfectly appropriate.

CONS

Sometimes she's also a perfect bore. If people saw the real her, they'd actually really like her.

The quilted Chanel bag belongs to one of two different types of women: the original and older sort, who is genuinely ladylike; and the newcomer, the younger fashionista, who has recognized that the world responds well to a lady and so has decided to act like one. Both types cultivate an image of old money, even if they grew up in working-class suburbs.

From her cashmere twinsets to her South Sea pearls, Chanel Bag Lady oozes class out of every double-stitched seam. At home she knows how to set the table; at work she effortlessly sets the agenda. Her girlfriends ask her for advice on the appropriate outfit for an event, and her colleagues ask her to head their charity committees.

Her attitude may be all blue blood, but she's more red-blooded than she'd ever admit. She'll fix herself a hot cup of English breakfast tea after she's had some even hotter sex. No, it won't have been with her husband; he'll have been far too busy at work with his secretary. It will have been with the spunky gardener at home waiting to mow her prize-winning hedges.

While her girlfriends can't decide between the salmon carpaccio with truffle oil and the tomato and mozzarella di bufala caprese salad, she knows exactly what she wants. She's known ever since she first subscribed to *Town and Country* magazine at the age of nine.

LOGO LUGGAGE LADY

Yes, the luggage costs more than most people's vacations, but that's the point. For Logo Lady, half the fun of traveling is watching people look on in envy as she nonchalantly identifies her designer bags on the luggage carousel, leaving others to desperately try to decipher which tattered black bag belongs to them. (And that's only if she's been forced to fly "commercial.")

She's the first-class fashionista who orders a Bloody Mary on arriving at Heathrow and slips on a pair of oversized dark shades just in case the paparazzi remembered to show up. When this woman says she means business, don't even suggest flying economy.

Logo Girl aspires to greatness, though not necessarily in the most noble of areas. She'll aim to own the most expensive shoes, receive the most party invites, become the most photographed nobody, gain the world record for the most air kisses per minute. She laughs louder, flies farther, and shops longer than mere mortals have the will or the right to do. And though she may not be a classic beauty, her confidence, warmth, and va-va-voom will make any party hush as she walks into the room.

She was born a star, and even if her face doesn't so much as make the cover of the local paper, she will die a star. Not content with the constant dull glow of life on Earth, she sparkles brighter and fades sooner. She'll be going out with a full face of makeup and a coy, well-rehearsed final remark.

PROS

She knows how to "work it."

CONS

Too much networking and not enough working. Sometimes you schmooze and you still lose.

HOLLYWOOD Bag Lady

Jennifer Lopez

OVER-STUFFED BAG LADY

PROS

She shows a selfless strength.

CONS

Martyrdom is so passé.

One look at this overstuffed bag and you needn't be religious to believe that martyrdom is still alive, if not doing so well. This is the bag of the woman who puts everything before herself, including a cart filled with cut-price deli meats as she walks through the supermarket aisles. The longer the bag's straps, the bigger the lady—in fact, if the straps extend below her waist, she probably doesn't have one.

The Overstuffed Bag Lady has a million different sections into which she can compartmentalize a dreary life. A worn wallet goes in the front pocket, a shopping list in the back, an unpaid school bill in the middle, and a tube of antacids on the side. With all her burdens and commitments, she must be careful to leave a little space for herself.

What this lady lacks in style, she more than makes up for in substance, size 16 pants aside. She is the friend you grasp for when your trendy "clutches" have let you go. Unpretentious, often underappreciated, she is the silent pillar of strength upon which the family unit rests. She's the woman who sees the value in bringing homemade snacks to the movies and putting the money she's saved toward her kids' Christmas presents.

Don't be fooled by her distinctive absence of glamour; beneath the buckled leather breathes the spirit of a goddess. She possesses a rich sense of humor in her full-figured body. But it's time she reminded her man that she's actually a woman and started making love instead of sandwiches.

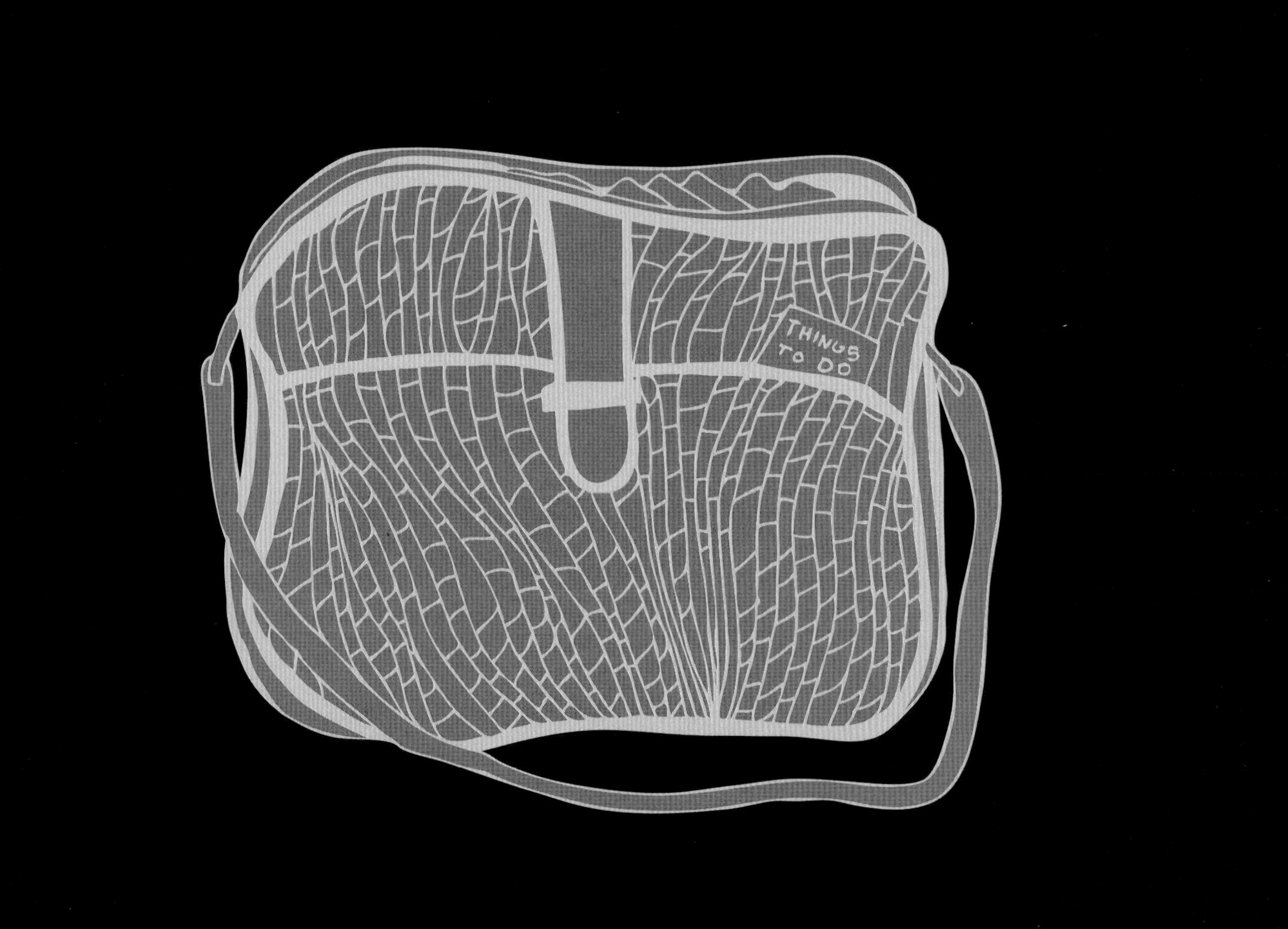
THINGS
TO DO

MINK PURSE LADY

From the slopes of St. Moritz to the shores of St. Tropez, she's the jet-setting princess flying first class all the way. With expensive tastes and an expense account to boot, she's living the high life while someone else picks up the check.

Her girlfriends are her shopping companions, her coconspirators, and her competition for male attention. They're just there to fill the empty days, while her much-older husband goes to work. From her salmon to her Marlboro Lights, her diet is entirely smoked. When your body is your business, it's better for both your figure and your figures to inhale rather than ingest.

Instead of being a working woman, Mink Minx has dedicated her professional life to "working" men. She knows just how to flutter her eyelashes and tilt her head. This glamourpuss is really an alley cat purring for her warm saucer of milk, but instead of sporting a mangy coat, her fur is from Escada.

Mink has turned her heart into a commodity and divorce into a profession; she's motivated by money, fame, and having the right last name. Why share toast and peanut butter with the one you love when you can eat Beluga caviar alone?

However cool she appears, it would be wrong to accuse her of having an icy heart. In truth, she's romantic to the bone; it's just that true love has caused her heartache, while false affections have brought her a country home.

PROS

Groomed to perfection, she's a fine piece of art in a connoisseur's collection.

CONS

Collectors don't stop looking once they've found their perfect piece. Who will keep her warm at night once she's taken off her mink?

HOLLYWOOD Bag Lady

Sharon Stone

FRENCH BASKET LADY

PROS

She knows that the fastest way to a man's heart is through his stomach. One bite and you're hers.

CONS

Men want to make her their wife as well as their mistress.

HOLLYWOOD Bag Lady

Nigella Lawson

She greets you with an open-armed "*Ciao!*" and a kiss on both cheeks. She drinks a milky full-fat cappuccino instead of a skim Starbucks version. She's impeccably groomed, managing to look earthy and glamorous at once: she's all sensual lips and womanly hips. Her beige linen pants float breezily around her olive legs, and cream suede loafers adorn her butter-soft feet.

She's well-practiced in the subtle art of femininity, managing to radiate both a motherly comfort and a sex-goddess aura, a combination men find irresistible. She's the mom all her son's school friends want to come home to devour for afternoon snack.

Even when running simple errands, such as buying antipasto at the local delicatessen, she uses the tricks her mother taught her—the power of a well-arched eyebrow, a hint of cleavage, and the promise of a home-cooked meal (even if it's not always her home that it's been cooked in).

Just as she'd never dream of running after the chicken she plans to roast in a honey marinade, she'd never chase a man either. Instead, she lures him with all things sticky and sweet and then has him for breakfast.

Basket Lady has cosmopolitan flair and a knowing smile that instantly puts people at ease. She's a great judge of character and has an innate sense of style; she can turn a small business into a bubbling cash flow, or a tiny café into the chicest spot in town.

HERMÈS KELLY BAG LADY

"I'm rich, I'm powerful, and I sure did marry well." This is what the Kelly bag says, elegantly dangling from a manicured fist. When Kelly Lady walks into a room, people make way. At a party everyone knows Kelly Lady has "arrived" even if she's a no-show.

While she might have been born into privilege, she secured the corner office by out-styling and out-slimming her competition. She's the über-chic urban hustler with the grooming of an heiress, who's more fearful of white bread than white supremacy. She's a perfectionist who fearlessly and masterfully deals with confrontation and office politics—and that's just her ordering a nonfat latte.

Pity the fool who ever tries mugging Kelly. From her lethally spiked Manolo Blahnik heels to her razor-sharp ghd-straightened bob, this woman is as much fatale as she is femme. She is focused and knows exactly who to do over to get the job done. She's the ultimate power player in the perfect Bill Blass suit, who is permanently dressed for lunch but never eats any.

You'll recognize Kelly Lady because she'll be immaculately groomed and will rarely carry any other bag, even if her leather trophy is an ugly shade of plum. Since she's spent six months on a waiting list and six months' pay on it, she'll be holding this old bag until she becomes one.

PROS

She's a walking fashion icon.

CONS

She can be about as warm as a New York winter. She shouldn't sacrifice her soul for style.

HOLLYWOOD Bag Lady

Victoria Beckham

HEMP SACK LADY

PROS

It is easy to fight for oneself. To fight for an ideology is where nobility lies.

CONS

Ideology and hypocrisy are best of friends.

HOLLYWOOD Bag Lady

Darryl Hannah

She is your hippie-chick flower child with fennel weaved through her flowing hair. She's the best friend you had in college with whom you no longer have anything in common—this is partly a sweet relief and partly a shame, because you sense something of value inside you died along with your friendship.

She drifts through people's lives, including her own, leaving only a whiff of tea-tree oil and a reminder of why aluminum-free deodorant never took off. Hemp Femme may not have showered for a fortnight, but she can campaign for "clean air" without a hint of irony. She possesses a naive piety, saving the "save the forest" mantra for her armpits while she hands out paper flyers.

This vegan idealist hasn't a spiteful bone in her calcium-depleted body. She's a great person with whom to share a philosophical conversation and an organic naturally decaffeinated soy cappuccino. Always a health-food nut, she will tell you she's wheat- and dairy-intolerant as she pinches bits of your chocolate chip brownie.

Hempy is so in touch with her "inner-self" she's lost touch with reality. When she tells you she's going to "save the planet," you just hope she means this one.

SAVE
THE
PLANET

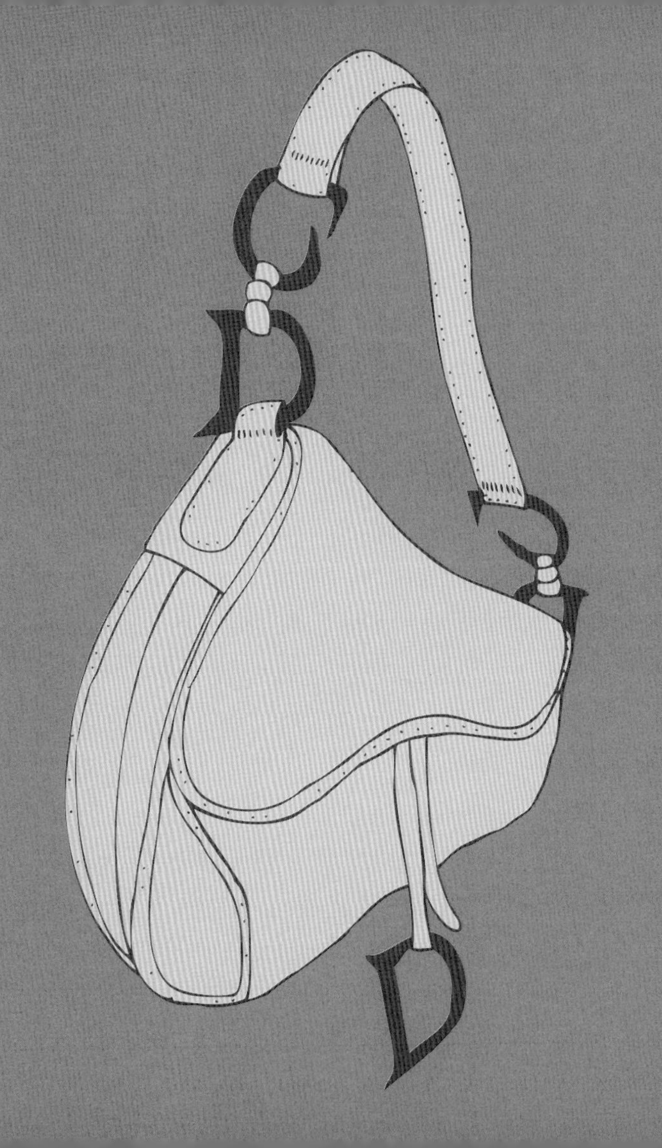

DIOR SADDLEBAG LADY

Down but not out. Low-key but high fashion. Cleverly borrowing from the past and reinventing it for the future, contemporary Saddle Girl has replaced the equestrian club with the nightclub.

Once the bag of the show jumper, it's now the must-have accessory for the young showstopper. These days Miss Saddlebag's only encounter with anything horse is her throat after a big night out; the only mules she knows about are the shoes in her closet. She might have left the stables behind, but she is just as feisty a competitor as ever, especially when it comes to men. Once she's set her mind on riding the prize stallion, you won't see her handing out carrots to donkeys.

As with the gaucho—Argentina's most daring and reckless herders for whom the saddle was their greatest trophy—today's Saddlebag Woman is brave, unapologetic for her talents, and made of rawhide.

From her NARS makeup to her Sigerson Morrison knee-length boots, it's dressage to impress. Dior Kid likes nothing more than a day of senseless spending with the sort of best friends that fit neatly into her wallet—Visa and Amex. Though she doesn't like her look to scream "expensive," she doesn't mind if it hints at it.

PROS

Despite the fashion fluff, she's a generous friend to have in your stable.

CONS

She may no longer ride horses, but her tongue is still whip sharp.

FENDI SPY BAG LADY

PROS

Cool has not left the building.

CONS

Sometimes you might wish it had.

HOLLYWOOD Bag Lady

Nicole Richie

The girl carrying the Fendi Spy Bag is not just a spy, she's a true fashion insider. She's visited the shows in Paris or New York, or at least feels like she has as a result of having her television being permanently tuned to Fashion TV. She's been lulled into a fashion trance, believing models to be the rule rather than the exception, and Diet Coke to be a legitimate source of nutrition. Don't be surprised if you hear her whispering "D*aaaa*rling" in her sleep as she double-kisses her pillow.

Spy Girl oozes a relaxed coolness yet is such a formidable dresser that when you see her out she makes you want to go home and get changed. She's a career girl, but you won't see her standing behind a counter or tied to a desk job. This girl works in a "studio," be it fashion or photo. She has long girly Friday lunch "meetings" at restaurants you'd go to for birthday and anniversary celebrations. And she can get in just about anywhere because she's friends with the PR girls who secretly run the city.

Every element of this girl's life is top shelf, though she'd get her assistant to reach up and grab it for her. You could call her pampered, you could call her spoiled to the core, but unless she thinks you're "connected" enough to give you her mobile number, you probably won't be able to call her at all.

When it comes to love, she's loyal and sweet—just as long as you take her to Portofino for summers and view buying her flowers as an everyday practice rather than a special treat.

CHINESE SILK BAG LADY

Chinese Silk Bag Lady may be made of a delicate fabric, but she isn't afraid of roughing it. An independent spirit and a truly nomadic soul, she has explored the jungles of Thailand's Golden Triangle and soaked on Bali's humid shores. Though she has a perpetual golden glow, she's far lower maintenance than she appears, preferring a blissful $5 beach massage to a $150 facial at Bliss Spa.

She's used to traveling light, be it with a backpack on vacations or a small silk bag at night. No lipstick here; a tub of pawpaw lip ointment is more than enough. When you brush against the nape of her neck it's not Chanel No. 5 that's making you choke, but her "signature scent," patchouli essential oil.

Silky tries to avoid complexity, preferring the simple life: a single house key on a hand-braided leather key ring; a few ten-dollar bills tied together with an elastic hair band. Louis Vuitton wallets need not apply; she doesn't want to carry any baggage—even if it is designer.

She has a semiconventional career as a photographer or in the arts, being allergic to the nine-to-five grind. She's a hippie who pays her taxes. Terrified of slipping into what she calls the "numbness of corporate life," she's forever planning ways to escape, even if it's just from her own conventional core.

PROS

She's never done anything or -one for the money.

CONS

Just because you're looking at the stars, doesn't mean you're not sitting in the gutter.

HOLLYWOOD Bag Lady

Cameron Diaz

BEJEWELED BAG LADY

PROS

Finally, an intelligent conversationalist who will get your blood boiling and your heart racing.

CONS

She's smart but a tad too studied.

HOLLYWOOD Bag Lady

Meryl Streep

From the black Baccarat-crystal chandelier hanging in her foyer to the oriental orchids pouring from every vase in her home, Bejeweled Babe views opulent objects as priceless works of art, rather than pricey purchases. To this end, Bejeweled Woman considers herself more eccentric than indulgent. In truth, she's a delicious combination of the two.

She's the queen of unexpected sophistication, wild-haired with jewel-toned glasses perched precariously at the end of her refined nose. Her body is draped in embroidered silk and wrapped in a turquoise-and-crystal pashmina. She looks as though she's just stepped out of an impressionist's artwork: vivid in color and perfectly poised just left of center.

Her home is more modern art gallery than humble abode. On one wall hangs an original geisha kimono discovered on a trip to Japan, on another a limited-edition Roy Lichtenstein pop-art screen-printed cartoon. And just when you're convinced of her good taste, she will proudly point out the nude painting displayed above the mantelpiece of herself, post-breastfeeding. In fact, while she may be wearing silk stockings and suspenders, don't be surprised if she also goes braless. This blatant disregard for "age-appropriate" dressing proves both that a woman can be sexy at any age and that gravity exists.

She is too outspoken to be considered a "lady" (something she's most proud of). Years of reading Russian literature and world newspapers have sharpened her wit and her wiles.

BALENCIAGA BAG LADY

Here's a dirty, pretty thing walking through the urban jungle. She'll be wearing Paper Denim jeans tucked into suede knee-high platform boots, while her mobile phone will be delicately pressed against one large gold earring. She is the taste maker, the heartbreaker, whose fifth food group is caffeine and sixth sense is for vintage shopping. Balenciaga Lady inhales the images in *W* magazine as if they were Acqua di Parma, while sipping her peach-nectar Bellini and pondering the merits of Sardinia over Miami.

If the bag is the original, she's the trendsetter who prides herself on being at the cutting edge of fashion, knowing exactly what's hot and what's not in any given week. If it's a copy, she's trying harder than she really needs to. Both types are party princesses and heat-seeking missiles. Balenciaga Babe will double-kiss the doorman at Bungalow 8 as he whisks her and her posse past the masses. Hers is a life lived behind velvet robes.

And while she is light on her feet, perhaps no one except her shoe-repair guy knows just how heavy a weight she carries on her shoulders. Few know the pressures of perfection quite like her: the endless struggle between drinking four sugary cocktails and still having to fit into size 6 clothes the following day, or the difficulty of finding a man, her equal—someone international, cool but sweet, handsome, and rich but not arrogant. "Like, *pleeease*. Is that too much to ask for?!"

PROS

She's a barista of conversation, making it as light and fluffy as a really great cappuccino.

CONS

She needs a little less attitude and a lot more gratitude.

HOLLYWOOD Bag Ladies

The Olsen twins

LE SPORTSAC LADY

PROS

She's loud and proud.

CONS

Whatever happened
to nice and quiet?

HOLLYWOOD Bag Lady

Gwen Stefani

How is it that Le Sportsac Girl has a permanent tan and a never-fading smile? It's because she always looks on the sunny side of life.

She's an on-the-go kind of girl, jammed into a bright and bubbly package. She has a quirky outlook on life and believes that every day is worth celebrating. Hers is the voice you'll hear above everyone else's when "Happy Birthday" is being sung. She is the girl whose whole-hearted laugh will filter into your conversation from the other side of the room. One look at the woman with the technicolored dream tote and you know she's not afraid of attracting attention. Does she seek it? She'd say, "No," but in a loud voice.

Le Sportsac Girl has a great sense of humor, which is just as well since her bag looks more like a comic strip than a respectable accessory. While she looks like an acid flashback, she's precise and unexpectedly clear of mind. Her diary may be covered in stickers, but her appointments are timed down to the minute.

She's most likely a graphic designer or at least has a healthy interest in aesthetics; she is the urban warrior camouflaged in the mayhem of city scenes.

TODS

TODS TOTE LADY

PROS

An heirloom rose in a flower bed of carnations.

CONS

So delicate a flower requires constant maintenance and can wilt with overwatering or careless enthusiasm.

If you're feeling hot under the collar, let Tods Tote Lady pour you a cool glass of rosé: Let her light and breezy laughter aerate your mood. She's the hostess with the mostest (and I'm not just talking about her trust fund).

If you visit her home (or, rather, one of her homes), she'll cook you a meal that will make your mouth water, and nourish your mind with a sense of humor as dry as a bone. While she didn't attend a swish Swiss finishing school, she could easily teach at one. No woman is as finessed in the art of flattery as the Tote Lady; she knows just what to say to make you feel like the queen of the world, and she's convincing enough to make you believe she actually means it.

In truth, the Tote is a master in the art of deflection. After hours of conversation, you'll feel as though you are best friends, when in fact she's revealed none of her secrets and you have spilled your guts on her terrazzo floors.

Beneath her calm, crisp exterior is a lady sensitive and tender, but she needs to be treated with kid gloves. A lost angry word will not be lost on Tods; instead her resentment will be hidden from you, buried deep beneath her smile in a place you can't reach to get close enough to mend. But if treated right, she will make everyday life a work of art, one painted in subtle hues and gentle yet generous brushstrokes.

SATIN CLUTCH LADY

PROS

Old-world passion
and all that jazz.

CONS

Her version of love
is often two-dimensional.

HOLLYWOOD Bag Lady

Nicole Kidman

Clutch Lady possesses ambition of a predominantly social nature. Forget the stairmaster; the only workout she needs is social climbing.

Nothing is as likely to bring a rosy flush to her cheeks as the dream of marrying royalty, or, at least, those who are royally rich. She's the girl sitting at home on a Saturday night, painting her toenails, because she refuses to lower her standards and accept dates with "average guys." She's so busy waiting for her dreamboat to arrive, she risks missing the ride altogether.

Rather than having a drink at the local bar, her perfect night involves a seat at her man's charity gala dinner, a carriage (think Aston Martin), and a glass slipper (think a Jimmy Choo Swarovski crystal–studded stiletto).

She's more princess than pragmatist: Happily leaving her wallet at home, she'll never carry a bag so small that it can't contain her mandatory red lipstick. Her greatest aphrodisiac is fantasy, making the inevitably messy reality of love disappointing. Too many Jane Austen novels and the dangerous belief that a man's worth is akin to his net worth have made her heart a dark shade of red.

She's so attached to *The Rules* that she may remain a spinster forever. She's so picky about what she puts in her clutch that she risks never having anything near her crotch. But to seduce this siren, deliver long-stemmed red roses after your first kiss and a huge engagement rock after twelve months.

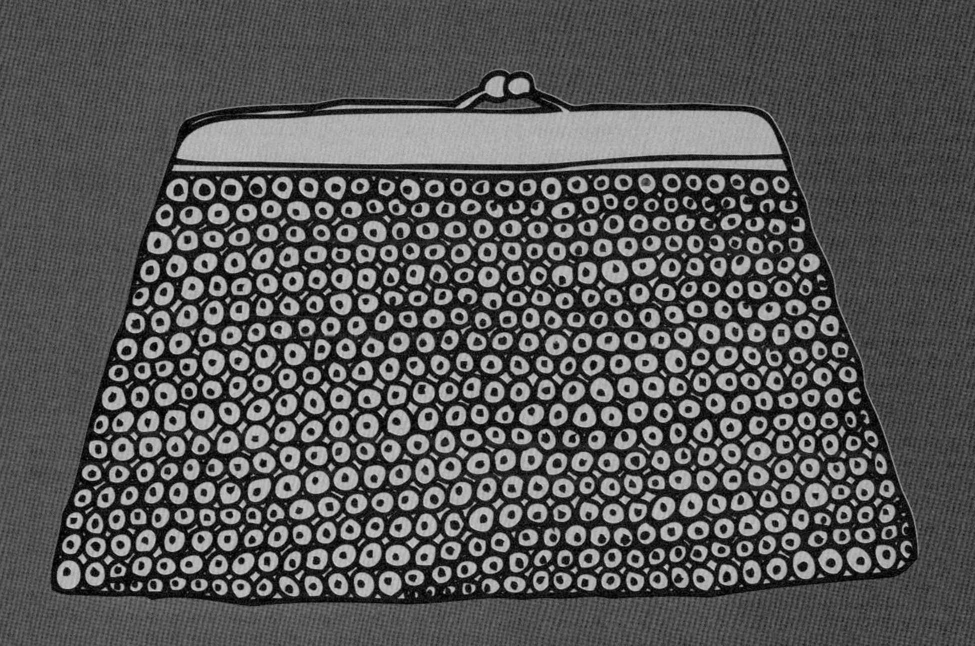

KE

GYM BAG LADY

Disciplined and determined, Gym Bag Girl is results oriented, unafraid of hard work, and perpetually "pumped" about being pumped. If you meet her for lunch, your meal is sure to be sprinkled with motivational mantras, rather than cheese.

She walks with a certain skip in her step. Perhaps it's because she's got her body fat down to 8 percent, perhaps it's a shortened ligament—either way she sure seems mighty pleased with herself.

Just as she targets specific muscle groups, Gym Bag Babe targets her men, but she'll miss a bull's-eye as frequently as she'll hit one (men are either terrified of, or turned on by, her strength, both the emotional and physical kinds). Gym Gal despises laziness almost as much as she does carbohydrates after 2 p.m. As a result, she needs a man who also wants to conquer the world one bench press at a time, a man who flexes his intellectual muscles with the same intensity as his forearms.

The problem with Gym Gal is that while she possesses great strength, she lacks subtlety, often delivering the brutal truth in a tone as hard as her glutes. She can "handle the truth," but she would have been too busy working out to have worked out that most other people can't. So while she hates excess glucose, sugarcoating some things may make her a little more popular with the girls at work.

PROS

She knows what she wants and goes after it.

CONS

If she's as hard on her friends as she is on herself, she may wind up very lonely. Occasionally she has to allow herself to deviate from her routine; flexibility is a crucial component of strength.

VINTAGE LEOPARD-PRINT LADY

PROS

She's a true original.

CONS

It's been said that originality is the art of concealing one's sources.

HOLLYWOOD Bag Lady

Dita Von Teese

You'll see her in a polka-dot singlet, high-waisted denim jeans, and fishnet stockings. Her platinum-blond tresses will be up in a 1940s do, her lips will be lacquered into a blood-red pout, her eyelids will be liquid lined, and her skin will reveal a cheeky Bettie Page tattoo. She's the free spirit who got lost somewhere between Jean Harlow and Rocky Horror, the consummate artist who uses her body as her canvas, telling the tale of her life with her cleverly crafted image. She's part screen siren, part street punk—a brazen girl hiding in the shadows of bright lights.

By day she works in a vintage-clothing store, selling pieces that have a history even more colorful than her own. By night she performs with her rock band—she's a wild cat unleashed on stage. While she may look like a loner, she seeks community more desperately than most. A girl who doesn't "fit in" is bound to fit just right with a group of "misfits."

Leopard-Print Princess looks to the past to get direction for the future, embracing it by reinventing it and, in the process, creating a history all of her own. She lives the sort of retro life that's only possible in a postmodern era.

She has a chip on her shoulder and a wiggle in her walk. She has abandoned society's "norms" and lives on her own terms. Her tiny, manic apartment downtown is as far as she can get from the suburban dream she has nightmares about.

HELLO KITTY BAG GIRL

Forget rose-tinted glasses; this girl sees life through techno-colored shades. She's optimistic to the point of naïveté. Nothing is serious to Hello Kitty Girl, and if it is, it's not for very long. The troubles of the world are fixed with a great movie, a piece of candy, and an off-pitch karaoke song.

Hello Kitty Kid has more energy than she knows what to do with—tapping her foot as she stands, shaking her leg as she sits. She wants the whole world to be a party and can't quite grasp the concept of despair; she's living in a pink helium balloon, while the rest of humanity gasps for air.

Using her fashion as a form of escapism, she blinds herself with positivity. Innocent, childlike clothes are the only items she wants to buy or see. It's as if she's playing a kooky character in a cartoon strip called *The World as It Should Be.*

From her crazy purple platform sneakers to her naughty schoolgirl braids, she's part impish chic, part freaky geek, but wholly redefining the modern world.

She communicates through instant messages, texting instead of talking. She has boyfriends she's never met before and a whole life lived in cyberspace.

PROS

The future is bright;
in fact, it's fluorescent pink.

CONS

Just because it's called virtual reality doesn't mean it's real.

DESIGNER BABY BAG LADY

PROS

Finally, she understands how much her own mother must love her.

CONS

When did going to the bathroom alone for four minutes become a luxury?

Her friends kindly call her a "yummy mommy," but after four hours' sleep and three diaper changes, she's never felt so yucky. Perhaps underneath the crayon-covered clothes and the dark circles, her friends have noticed an inner glow that's borne of a life with purpose—that purpose being her adorable little shits. Though she may be exhausted, she's as conscientious as ever, buying organic baby food and enrolling her two-year-old in figurative dance classes.

As she drifts deeper into little people's land, she finds she has less in common with her single friends. Like, have they always been so selfish? A part of her longs for freedom, but she's discovered a love so grounding that she's happily laid her wings to rest.

She considers herself a modern mother and had promised herself that she wouldn't be one of those ghastly women who never stop raving about how brilliant her child is. However, she justifiably broke that promise once she discovered how truly gifted her child was.

She has a newfound appreciation for firefighters and garbage men and all those who have 6 a.m. starts. Lying in bed, she spends the five seconds it takes before she passes out cold considering whether she should have another baby or hand in the current brood and flee to Mexico. If only someone had warned her how unrelenting motherhood would be, she'd have . . . done it anyway.

I'm NOT
A Plastic
bag

ETHICALLY CHIC BAG LADY

Forget ostrich, croc, or kidskin; this gal knows that ethics are officially in. You will find her at her local organic grocery store, sensually smelling the peaches and pressing the mangoes for firmness. Eco-Chic Chick finds the experience satisfies both her senses and her sense of right and wrong. She's also pleased to have discovered that she doesn't feel as guilty buying chocolate if it's labeled organic.

She considers herself spiritual, and after her weekly Pilates class feels closer to God, as well as those snug size 10 pants. Although she may be a tad vain, she has warm blood flowing through them. Always ready to offer a gentle smile or a generous embrace, she is a magnificent hostess, and you'd prefer to spend more time at her home than your own.

Most at peace when surrounded by close family and friends, she gives of herself so that others may feel at ease. But when all the guests have left, when she's washed up the last glass and cleared the leftovers into the compost bin, she sometimes wonders if her friends realize how much she's given up for them.

Ethically Chic Chick is passionate about doing the right thing and genuinely hopes to leave a better world for her children. She's a modern greenie who's willing to shorten the length of her beloved hot showers and change to energy-saving lightbulbs—as long as it doesn't ruin the look of her lamps. She'll happily switch to green power and stilettos if it helps to reduce her carbon footprint.

PROS

Thanks to her, green is the new black.

CONS

Don't just buy organic water; recycle the bottle.

ACKNOWLEDGMENTS

I'd like to thank the people who have always been there for me, no matter where I was.

To my mother, Sylvia Eisman, for her ingenious, unconventional wisdom, and unconditional love; my father, Peter Eisman, for proving that good men do exist, as do corny jokes; Daniel Eisman, for becoming a dear friend as well as a brother; Jacqui Foux, my big "shishta" with a huge heart and the most adorable little boys; and my grandparents, Eddie Reich, Nanny Eda, and Papa Harry, whose love of life lives in me.

To my dear friends Chevonne Silverman, Tali Shine, Ziah Lane, Marija Skara, Carlii Lyon, Pensiri Keller, Jourdan Krauss, and Marc Honaker, thank you for being my copassengers on this wild ride. I love you.

No one gets anywhere without a few people taking a chance on them. To my colleagues, bosses, and friends from Rockefeller Plaza to North Ryde, Park Avenue to Park Street, Woollahra to West Hollywood, I've enjoyed every minute working with you. My deepest gratitude to Al Zuckerman and Chris Schillig for bringing this quirky confection to life.

And a bright pink, fancy ribbon-tied thank-you to my darling, Siimon Reynolds. No matter which handbag I hold in my hand, you are the treasure I carry in my heart.

♥

Kathryn
Eisman

KATHRYN EISMAN is one of Australia's rising media stars. She is a renowned expert on style and culture, and her witty observations on modern life have been featured worldwide. She has worked as a reporter for NBC in New York and Foxtel in Australia, and has been a featured columnist in *Cleo*, *Men's Health*, and *Pinnacle* magazines. Kathryn is *Cosmopolitan* magazine's Fun Fearless Female Awards author of the year. Her previous book, *How to Tell a Man by His Shoes*, was an international best-seller, published in ten countries. She currently divides her time between Sydney, Los Angeles, and New York, where she spends far too much money on handbags.

COSMO
SAVE THE PLANET